GRAPHIC SCIENCE

ADVENTURES in SOUND

WITH MAX AXIOM SUPER SCIENTIST

by Emily Sohn

illustrated by Cynthia Martin
and Anne Timmons

Consultant:
Dr. Ronald Browne
Associate Professor of Elementary Education
Minnesota State University, Mankato

Capstone
press

Mankato, Minnesota

Graphic Library is published by Capstone Press,
151 Good Counsel Drive, P.O. Box 669, Mankato, Minnesota 56002.
www.capstonepub.com

Books published by Capstone Press are manufactured with paper
containing at least 10 percent post-consumer waste.

Library of Congress Cataloging-in-Publication Data
Sohn, Emily.
    Adventures in sound with Max Axiom, super scientist / by Emily Sohn; illustrated by
Cynthia Martin and Anne Timmons.
        p. cm.—(Graphic library. Graphic science)
    Summary: "In graphic novel format, follows the adventures of Max Axiom as he explains the
science behind sound"—Provided by publisher.
    Includes bibliographical references and index.
    ISBN-13: 978-0-7368-6836-5 (hardcover)
    ISBN-10: 0-7368-6836-4 (hardcover)
    ISBN-13: 978-0-7368-7889-0 (softcover pbk.)
    ISBN-10: 0-7368-7889-0 (softcover pbk.)
    1. Sound—Juvenile literature. 2. Adventure stories—Juvenile literature. I. Martin, Cynthia,
1961– ill. II. Timmons, Anne, ill. III. Title. IV. Series.
QC225.5.S64 2007
534—dc22   2006027995

Art Director and Designer
Bob Lentz

Cover Artist
Tod Smith

Colorist
Michael Kelleher

Editor
Christopher L. Harbo

Photo illustration credits: Scott Thoms/Capstone Press, 8 (bottom)

Printed in the United States of America in Stevens Point, Wisconsin.
062011   006228WZVMI

TABLE of CONTENTS

Do you see that? Vibrations cause invisible waves in the air, sort of like throwing a pebble causes ripples in a pond. These waves make up what we call sound.

SUBJECT: JACKHAMMER

MAX AXIOM

SOUND WAVES

When an object vibrates, it actually causes nearby air molecules to bounce against each other.

SUBJECT: JACKHAMMER

MAX AXIOM

Their motion causes other molecules to bounce too. This transfer of energy moves outward from the source of the sound, creating sound waves.

MOLECULES: Tiny particles that make up a substance

IMAGE ENHANCED

Of course, some sounds are louder than others. The difference is called intensity.

TWEET!

TWEET!

TWEET!

TATATATATAT!

Stronger vibrations are more intense. They cause louder sounds.

Loudness is also called volume. The higher the volume, the louder the sound.

PUTT PUTT PUTT

I have a job to do. Please, leave me alone.

PUTT PUTT PUTT PUTT

THE HUMAN LARYNX

ACCESS GRANTED: MAX AXIOM

EPIGLOTTIS

VOCAL CORDS

LARYNX

TRACHEA

Inside your throat, your larynx allows you to talk, sing, and make other noises. Inside the larynx, two muscles called vocal cords squeeze together and vibrate as air passes by them. The faster they vibrate, the higher your voice sounds. Your tongue and lips shape the sounds you make.

9

We've gone to the source of sound waves. Now, let's take a look at how these invisible waves turn into the sounds we hear.

Noise, noise. Who do these people think they are?

We hear through our ears, so let's take a look inside Al's ear.

Believe it or not, the folds and curves of the outer ear serve a purpose.

They collect sounds and funnel them into the ear.

OUTER EAR

MIDDLE EAR

INNER EAR

The ear canal is also part of the outer ear. It carries sounds to the middle ear just ahead.

WAX

EAR DRUM

HAMMER

ANVIL

In the middle ear, sounds vibrate the eardrum and three tiny bones called the hammer, anvil, and stirrup.

STIRRUP

Together, these parts make sounds louder before they are sent into the inner ear.

Vibrations from the stirrup travel to the snail-shaped cochlea in the inner ear.

Liquid in the cochlea gets wavy when vibrations arrive.

COCHLEA

These are hair cells inside the cochlea. They send electrical signals to the brain. The signals serve as messages that sound has arrived.

TO BRAIN

HAIR CELLS

13

The material sound travels through affects how you hear it.

GGBLUUUUWW

Yikes!

If you've ever listened to sounds underwater, you may know what I mean.

Hi, Max! Did you know that sound waves travel five times faster through water than through air?

Oh, yeah. It's also hard to tell which direction sounds are coming from underwater. That whale really took me by surprise!

It was probably talking to other whales. Many creatures use sound to communicate underwater.

That's cool! But I think I'll try to find someplace quieter.

Now we know where sounds come from and how we hear them. Let's check out what sound can do and what we can do with sound.

RRUMMBLE!

RRUMBLE!

CRACKK!

RUMBLE!

RUMBLE!

Uh, oh. There's a storm coming. Time to head indoors.

I'll just hop on this sound wave and take it for a ride.

MORE ABOUT SOUND

Sound travels faster through solids than through gases and liquids. Why? Because the molecules in solids are packed closer together. The closer the molecules, the faster the sound waves travel from one molecule to the next. A sound travels 770 miles (1,239 kilometers) per hour through air. It speeds through steel at about 11,630 miles (18,716 kilometers) per hour.

Most bats use echolocation to hunt. As they fly, bats release high-pitched sounds that bounce off objects all around them. Based on the echoes they hear, the bats can locate and determine the size of insects fluttering nearby.

The hammer, anvil, and stirrup are the smallest bones in the human body. They are the same size now as they were the day you were born. All together, they could fit on a penny.

Ear wax helps keep your ears clean. As wax forms inside the ear canal, it clings to dirt particles. Eventually, the wax works its way out of the ear, carrying the dirt along with it.

The liquid in the cochlea does more than just magnify vibrations. It also plays a role in balance and helps your body know what is up and what is down.

Elephants use infrasound, or sound below the range of human hearing, to talk to each other. They can use rumbling sounds as low as 5 Hz to communicate.

A cricket's hearing organs are located just below the knees of its front legs. A cicada's hearing organ is on its abdomen.

 Scientists measure the loudness, or volume, of sounds in decibels (dB). A whisper measures about 20 dB, while normal talking is 60 dB. A jet measures about 120 dB and a firecracker exploding is about 140 dB. Any sound above 85 dB can cause hearing damage if listened to for too long. At close range, noise levels above 140 dB cause immediate hearing damage.

 Blue whales are the loudest animals on earth. Their calls have measured 188 dB and can be heard from hundreds of miles away.

MORE ABOUT

SUPER SCIENTIST

Real name: Maxwell J. Axiom
Hometown: Seattle, Washington
Height: 6' 1"   **Weight:** 192 lbs
Eyes: Brown   **Hair:** None

Super capabilities: Super intelligence; able to shrink to the size of an atom; sunglasses give x-ray vision; lab coat allows for travel through time and space.

Origin: Since birth, Max Axiom seemed destined for greatness. His mother, a marine biologist, taught her son about the mysteries of the sea. His father, a nuclear physicist and volunteer park ranger, schooled Max on the wonders of earth and sky.

One day on a wilderness hike, a megacharged lightning bolt struck Max with blinding fury. When he awoke, Max discovered a newfound energy and set out to learn as much about science as possible. He traveled the globe earning degrees in every aspect of the field. Upon his return, he was ready to share his knowledge and new identity with the world. He had become Max Axiom, Super Scientist.

GLOSSARY

absorb (ab-ZORB)—to soak up

cochlea (KOH-klee-uh)—a spiral-shaped part of the ear that helps send sound messages to the brain

decibel (DESS-uh-bel)—a unit for measuring the volume of sounds

eardrum (IHR-druhm)—a thin piece of skin stretched tight like a drum inside the ear; the eardrum vibrates when sound waves strike it.

echolocation (eh-koh-loh-KAY-shuhn)—the process of using sounds and echoes to locate objects; bats use echolocation to find food.

energy (EN-ur-jee)—the ability to do work, such as moving things or giving heat or light

frequency (FREE-kwuhn-see)—the number of sound waves that pass a location in a certain amount of time

hertz (HURTS)—a unit for measuring the frequency of sound wave vibrations; one hertz equals one sound wave per second.

molecule (MOL-uh-kyool)—two or more atoms of the same or different elements that have bonded; a molecule is the smallest part of a compound that can be divided without a chemical change.

pitch (PICH)—the highness or lowness of a sound; low pitches have low frequencies and high pitches have high frequencies.

reflect (ri-FLEKT)—to bounce off an object

refract (ri-FRACT)—to bend when passing through a material at an angle

vibration (vye-BRAY-shuhn)—a fast movement back and forth

Read More

Bayrock, Fiona. *Sound: A Question and Answer Book.* Questions and Answers: Physical Science. Mankato, Minn.: Capstone Press, 2006.

Cooper, Christopher. *Sound: From Whisper to Rock Band.* Science Answers. Chicago: Heinemann, 2004.

Dreier, David Louis. *Sound.* Science around Us. Chanhassen, Minn.: Child's World, 2005.

Parker, Steve. *Making Waves: Sound.* Everyday Science. Chicago: Heinemann, 2005.

Trumbauer, Lisa. *All about Sound.* Rookie Read-About Science. New York: Children's Press, 2004.

Internet Sites

FactHound offers a safe, fun way to find Internet sites related to this book. All of the sites on FactHound have been researched by our staff.

Here's how:
1. Visit *www.facthound.com*
2. Choose your grade level.
3. Type in this book ID **0736868364** for age-appropriate sites. You may also browse subjects by clicking on letters, or by clicking on pictures and words.
4. Click on the **Fetch It** button.

FactHound will fetch the best sites for you!

INDEX